my home in the desert

By J. Patrick Lewis

Children's Press®
An Imprint of Scholastic Inc.

Library of Congress Cataloging-in-Publication Data

Names: Lewis, J. Patrick.
Title: My home in the desert/by J. Patrick Lewis.
Description: New York, NY : Children's Press, [2017] | Series: Rookie poetry.
Animal homes | Includes index.
Identifiers: LCCN 2016030841| ISBN 9780531228715 (library binding) | ISBN
9780531230060 (pbk.)
Subjects: LCSH: Desert animals—Juvenile literature.
Classification: LCC QL116 .L49 2017 | DDC 591.754—dc23
LC record available at https://lccn.loc.gov/2016030841

Produced by Spooky Cheetah Press
Design by Anna Tunick

All rights reserved. Published in 2017 by Children's Press, an imprint of Scholastic Inc.
Printed in China 62

SCHOLASTIC, CHILDREN'S PRESS, ROOKIE POETRY™, and associated logos
are trademarks and/or registered trademarks of Scholastic Inc.

1 2 3 4 5 6 7 8 9 10 R 26 25 24 23 22 21 20 19 18 17

Photos ©: cover snake: Rolf Nussbaumer Photography/Alamy Images; cover background: Givaga/iStockphoto; back cover
meerkat: kristianbell/Getty Images; back cover scorpion: Mikhail Egorov/Shutterstock, Inc.; back cover camel: LucVi/Shutterstock,
Inc.; back cover background: FRIEDRICHSMEIER/Alamy Images; cloud vector throughout: Freepik.com; 1: Michael Marquand/Getty
Images; 2-3: Martin Harvey/Getty Images; 5: Anton Petrus/Shutterstock, Inc.; 7: Steve & Dave Maslowski/Getty Images; 9 background:
FRIEDRICHSMEIER/Alamy Images; 9 meerkats: kristianbell/Getty Images; 11 sky: Realimage/Alamy Images; 11 main: Rick & Nora Bowers/
Alamy Images; 11 cactus: Dmitry/Fotolia; 13 background: FLPA/Alamy Images; 13 main: Mikhail Egorov/Shutterstock, Inc.; 14-15 left camel: LucVi/
Shutterstock, Inc.; 15 right camel: Bernd Bieder/Getty Images; 15 background: Michael Marquand/Getty Images; 17 main: Joel Sartore/Getty Images;
17 sky: Martin Harvey/Getty Images; 19 meerkats: Thomas Dressler/Getty Images; 19 hare: Robert J. Ross/Getty Images; 19 background: Markus
Obländer/Getty Images; 19 camel: LucVi/Shutterstock, Inc.; 19 scorpion: Mikhail Egorov/Shutterstock, Inc.; 19 roadrunner: Steve & Dave Maslowski/
Getty Images; 19 sidewinder: Rick & Nora Bowers/Alamy Images; 20 left, center right plants: photka/Thinkstock; 20 center left plant: sirichai2514/
Depositphotos; 20 right plant: vaccnma/Depositphotos; 20 sidewinder: Rick & Nora Bowers/Alamy Images; 20 roadrunner: Steve & Dave Maslowski/
Getty Images; 20 meerkats: Thomas Dressler/Getty Images; 21 center right plant: manub/Depositphotos; 21 left plant: vaeenma/Depositphotos; 21
center left plant: DNY59/Getty Images; 21 right plant: Dmitry/Fotolia; 21 scorpion: Mikhail Egorov/Shutterstock, Inc.; 21 camel: LucVi/Shutterstock,
Inc.; 21 hare: Robert J. Ross/Getty Images; 23 center bottom: jacobeukman/Thinkstock; 23 bottom: Anton Petrus/Shutterstock, Inc.; 23 center: Markus
Obländer/Getty Images; 23 center top: Michael Marquand/Getty Images; 23 top: Mikhail Egorov/Shutterstock, Inc.

table of contents

welcome to the desert

Every bug, **rodent**, rabbit, and rattler
in our **habitat** soaks up the sun.
If you would like to meet in the shimmering
heat of the desert, come join in the fun!

4

The world's deserts cover about one-third of Earth's surface.

roadrunner

I am a bird who enjoys going "cuckoo"
for the lizards and snakes I devour.
But I much prefer sprinting to flying:
I can run twenty miles per hour!

meerkat

My family of twenty or more
is known as a "gang" or a "mob."
We watch out for eagles and jackals
and cobras because that's our job.

sidewinder rattlesnake

america

EST. 1776

I make lines like zigzaggy S's
on **dunes** along this golden land.
When my belly is full, then I wind up
and disappear deep in the sand.

scorpion

I may seem like a miniature lobster but my **burrow** is not in the ocean. What accounts for my fearsome appearance are my looks and my locomotion!

camel

The Dromedary has one hump,
　　the Bactrian has two.
It is easy to forget this rule,
　　so here is what to do:
Roll the Bactrian on its back behind:
over on its back behind:
The Dromedary is different
　　from the Bactrian kind.

14

black-tailed jackrabbit

Ask a hawk, owl, fox, or coyote,
"Name your favorite fast-food dessert."
They will say the "American desert hare"—
That is me! I am on constant alert!

hidden homes

In this **vast** playground of wind and sky, you are bound to discover a friend or two, but it may take a while and a very sharp eye to see shy desert animals come into view.

fact files

	Roadrunner	Meerkat	Sidewinder Rattlesnake
HOW BIG AM I?	about 22 inches tall *(twice as tall as a robin)*	about 12 inches tall *(the same as a ruler)*	up to 32 inches long *(almost as long as a yardstick)*
HOW MUCH DO I WEIGH?	about 10 ounces *(six candy bars)*	about 2 pounds *(two soccer balls)*	1 pound *(a football)*
WHAT DO I EAT?	small mammals, reptiles, insects	insects, fruit, lizards, birds	rodents, lizards, birds

Scorpion	Camel **Dromedary & Bactrian**	Black-Tailed Jackrabbit
up to 12 inches long *(as long as a ruler)*	up to 6.6 **(D)** or 5.9 **(B)** feet tall at the shoulder *(taller than some grown-ups)*	up to 2 feet tall *(two rulers)*
up to 3.5 ounces *(a deck of cards)*	up to 1,500 pounds **(D)** or 1,100 pounds **(B)** *(about three times as much as a gorilla)*	up to 9 pounds *(about the same as a housecat)*
insects	grasses, plants	grasses, cacti and other plants

deserts...the dry facts

1. **A desert does not have to be hot.** It just has to be dry! There are two types of deserts on Earth: hot and cold. Hot deserts sometimes get small amounts of rain. Cold deserts get small amounts of snow.

2. **The world's largest cold desert is Antarctica.** The coldest temperature ever recorded there was -135.8°Fahrenheit (-94.7°Celsius). Just imagine: Your freezer is 0°Fahrenheit (-18°Celsius). Antarctica is 135 degrees colder!

3. **The world's largest hot desert is the Sahara in northern Africa.** It is about as big as the entire United States.

4. **Hot desert plants are used to living with small amounts of water.** They spread their roots out very wide just under the soil, and have very small leaves. This helps them conserve water.

5. **An oasis is a small area of standing water surrounded by hot desert.** Travelers and animals love to rest and drink water under the shade of its trees and plants!

glossary

burrow (BUR-oh): A tunnel or hole in the ground made or used as a home by a rabbit or other animal.

dunes (DOONZ): Small hills formed by the wind or tides.

habitat (HAB-uh-tat): The place where a plant or animal usually lives or grows.

rodent (ROH-duhnt): A small mammal with large, sharp front teeth that constantly grow and are used for gnawing.

vast (VAST): Very large in extent or amount.

index

facts for now

Visit this Scholastic Web site to le... ...ut deserts an...
the Teaching Guide for this series: www.factsfornow.schol...
Enter the keyword **Deserts**

about the author

J. Patrick Lewis has published 100 children's picture and poetry
books to date, with a wide variety of publishers. The Poetry
Foundation named him the third U.S. Children's Poet Laureate.